FRITZ KÜHN / WROUGHT IRON

FRITZ KÜHN

WROUGHT IRON

G E O R G E G. H A R R A P & C O. L T D, L O N D O N

Translated by
CHARLES B. JOHNSON

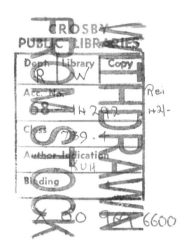

Copyright by Verlag Ernst Wasmuth Tübingen
First English Edition 1965 by
George G. Harrap & Co Ltd London
Printed and bound by Ensslin-Druck Reutlingen
Printed in Germany

FOREWORD

Various reasons prompted me to make available to the public this book, now in its tenth (German) edition, of the works of the outstandingly gifted master-craftsman in wrought iron, Fritz Kühn. Being aware of the desire of many architects for a graphic illustrated account of wrought iron, it seemed to me a specially happy coincidence that I could fulfil this wish and at the same time present an artistically gifted master conversant with every aspect of his craft who, building on his technical knowledge, develops designs and shows in his creations a clear-cut composition. Kühn is familiar with the works of the past, but seeks to do justice to the stylistic perception of our own times, and it seems to me that in this he has been remarkably successful. The close link with Nature, which will quickly become apparent to everyone who looks through the pages of this book, endows his work with a special charm. And in this connection it is noteworthy that Karl Blossfeldt's book Urformen der Kunst ('Ancestral Forms of Art') has provided Fritz Kühn, as he himself says, with numerous ideas. The fact that he was able to reproduce in iron many of the motifs in that book demonstrates how important was the work of Professor Blossfeldt who, by enlarging even the smallest parts of flowers, afforded an insight into the secrets of Nature. And through these motifs he consciously strove to stimulate art and handicraft. Another factor which induced me to proceed with this publication was that Fritz Kühn himself photographed nearly all his works, showing himself in the process to be an outstanding photographer. Because he knows his own works better than anyone else, he knows which in each case are the dominant features, and so can make use of photographic detail to give a close insight into the designs. The iron takes on a living form, the eye rejoices not only at the design but also the skill with which it has been executed. In a real sense one experiences the forging, the processes become intelligible, one senses the creative hand and sees the hammer-blows; one realizes the possibilities of designing in iron. Most of Fritz Kühn's creations were designed by himself, the rest in conjunction with architects. Throughout he proceeds only from legitimate uses of iron and has always been careful not to violate them; and it is from this that the naturalness and vitality so evident in his work derive. If the happy blending of masterly ability and exquisite feeling for form displayed here continues to exert its influence, the aim of this book will have been fulfilled.

Günther Wasmuth

Gate and screens, Freiburg Cathedral, Saxony.

WROUGHT IRON

Wrought iron is the material of the smith; bars of it are delivered to him from the rolling-mill, mainly in the form of round, square, and flat bars of varying dimensions. Characterized by its strength and solidity, wrought iron is specially suitable for structures intended to support, separate or screen, or to protect people's homes. Such structures can be made from standard sections of the material with little effort or knowledge of technical procedure; they are then for the most part tasteless and lifeless. But they can also assume vigorous form by means of beautiful and expressive designs achieved by forging – i. e., by hammering the material while at a heat suitable for a particular job.

Every design after which we strive is circumscribed by laws we must observe; for in the world of design, as in life, certain laws apply, and these must be thoroughly understood by the master-craftsman. The first prerequisite for producing a good, irreproachable piece of wrought ironwork must be to give vital form to the iron by means of simple yet technically proper designs. By 'technically proper' is meant mastering the techniques of forging and applying them correctly. These techniques of forging are: drawing out, upsetting or jumping up, joining and separating, punching, chiselling and splitting, rolling and bending, grooving and ribbing, cleaning off, fire welding, riveting and collaring. Furthermore the smith must know the properties of his material – viz., its degree of hardness and toughness. The design emerges from the way in which the material is fashioned. A simple, clearly evolved design obliges its designer to be accurate in the execution of it, for a simple design inevitably reveals any technical or structural defects. As it is the tendency in every healthy development to progress from the simple to the more complex, only those who have applied the principles of good taste and artistry and have mastered a simple design should attempt another of richer or more complex character. To apply such principles to a design means to look into its inner distinctive nature; but to do this the craftsman in wrought iron must have mastered all the basic aspects of his craft, while the outsider must have acquired at least a partial understanding of them. One must, by means of careful consideration of a particular design, be able to see in the mind's eye its further development and formation, for only then will a piece of work yield what it is capable of yielding. While it is true that aesthetic appreciation is more or less innate in human beings, it must nevertheless be developed.

Artistically forged designs must be creatively fashioned from one's own aesthetic sense; only in this way can the complete work achieve individuality and its true worth, only then will it bear the stamp of the master's personality. It is therefore wrong to imitate the decorative motifs of others and to incorporate them into one's own work. Apart from the consideration that it is purely a matter of luck whether these motifs will be at all appropriate, conceived as they were for a different piece of work, with a definite purpose and application in mind, the imitator will do himself a great deal of harm, for when tackling another piece of work he will come to grief and be revealed as an ignorant opportunist. A craftsman who aims to create work of enduring merit must have character and self-respect; he must love his craft and be dedicated to it body and soul. It may happen, for example, that for a certain grille the decorative motifs have to be forged several times before the right effect is achieved, with a consequent loss of time and earnings. How strong the temptation is in such cases to produce a worthless instead of a worthwhile finished article! It is a matter which calls for pride in one's work and in oneself.

Collaboration between architect and craftsman is of considerable importance, because the architect rarely possesses as great a knowledge of the materials used as does the craftsman, while the latter, for his part, must, if for instance he is making a set of railings, work within the context of the general architectural plan. In such circumstances collaboration and mutual trust yield good results. If an archi-

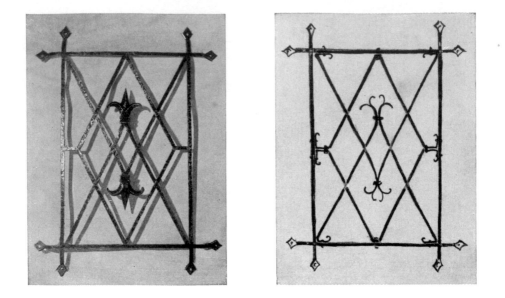

tect is not conversant with the material and techniques, he should not draw the designs of the wrought ironwork himself, but call in the craftsman to help him. There are, on the other hand, many masters who lack the courage to draw the architect's attention to possible defects in the drawing. It is specially wrong of an architect, however, to disregard helpful suggestions and insist on a precise interpretation of his design, for then technical aids must often be employed which impair the character of a correct and good piece of work and render it worthless. A certain measure of freedom in the execution of detail must on principle be allowed the craftsman. If, on the other hand, the architect entrusts the craftsman not only with the detail but also with the design, it may well happen that the craftsman, while able to cope with his own side of the work, will fail to appreciate the structure as a whole and the scale to which he should work. He may, indeed, be without feeling for architecture; if so, the result can only be failure. In both cases the blame is shared by the architect and the craftsman.

If because of an extensive building programme there is a heavy demand for wrought-iron articles, this should not be made the excuse for second-rate work. Buying machine-pressed leaves and rosettes ready-made from a dealer, riveting them to a piece of ironwork and then passing it off as a piece of craftsmanship is fraud and destroys the capacity for appraising a really good piece of craftsmanship. It was this kind of procedure which once led to the decline of our craft. Consider the following example: a locksmith received an order to manufacture some door panels in wrought iron in accordance with specifications supplied (see above, left). By making a literal interpretation of the specifications the firm behaved unscrupulously, neglecting to draw the architect's attention to the technical defects in it. They nevertheless accepted the order – even though they had no notion of how to produce decorative wrought ironwork. To give the impression of wrought iron, the iron was disguised by hammer bruises. For the two ornaments, which were to grow out of the bars (the collars, also marked on the design, were intended to hold the ends of the bars in position), a model was made by the firm and, because several panels of identical design were to be made, the ornaments were cast accordingly. All the parts were then joined by oxy-acetylene welds, and when in position were again hammered. Such work has absolutely nothing in common with craftsmanship in wrought iron. I have by way of contrast sketched this panel with the same basic design but taking into account the various forging and other technical requirements for the job (see above, right). The use of this design would certainly not have cost much more, but would undoubtedly have improved the result.

A great deal of bad workmanship can be attributed to the fact that jobs are offered out on tender, which means that the orders for them go mostly to the lowest bidder. Artistically designed wrought ironwork is always a matter of mutual trust, both as to the execution and the pricing. It is for this reason that the placing of orders should be by private treaty. The responsibility for this rests largely with the architect, whose duty it is to enlighten the building owner about the peculiar nature of good-quality wrought ironwork and to interest him in it. No architect should sanction a showy piece of work which not only is cheap but looks cheap, since work of a high standard of craftsmanship can be produced at competitive prices. This too can be exemplified: the illustrations here show two panels which were designed and executed on the same principle and which differ only in that one is more expensive than the other. Both solutions are good and of lasting value. That is why tenders should only be made on the basis of the design and the work carried out; the price can of course be estimated in advance. The tender would then be a contest to see who could get the best results. It should also be mentioned that it is extremely important for the craftsman to be told how much money is available for a given piece of work, so that he can be guided by this know-

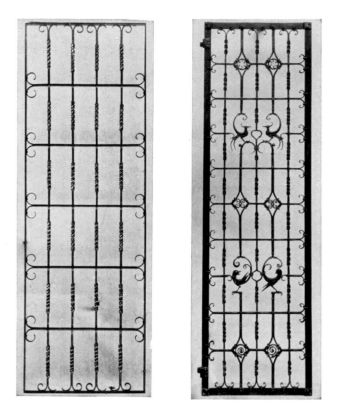

ledge from the outset, at the design stage. An architect's design, like a craftsman's execution of it, is subject to laws.

Even though the major techniques of forging have for the most part remained unchanged, a piece of decorative wrought ironwork executed today should not resemble those of the past. This mistake is nevertheless often made, simply because work is produced following old patterns and outmoded styles. To achieve a contemporary look, three points must be observed, and these are very important: a thorough knowledge of the material to be fashioned and of its technicalities – for it is out of the material and its fashioning that the design evolves; creative ability, feeling for form, and good taste; and an awareness of the spirit of the times. Clear thinking and logical development must go hand in hand with imagination. The examples shown here were designed and executed on these principles, and yet they are all basically different. They were in every case fashioned with reference to a given building and its particular requirements and to the place where they were to be installed. A gate with whimsical animal motifs, for example, would not be used at the front of a dignified residence. When making out a design I proceed as follows: first of all, the best means of incorporating a required item of decorative wrought ironwork into the general architecture can be enlivened most effectively by means of a richly fashioned grille, whilst a grille which in its basic features is simple and uncomplicated can often provide a beneficial contrast to more strongly motivated structural forms. I then consider the purpose for which the grille is intended and formulate the design most suitable to interpret these requirements. In this way the groundwork for the fashioning of a given piece of work follows a natural progression, with the result that even elaborately decorated and vigorously executed ironwork can impart visual serenity. Good ironwork of the past can provide us with useful suggestions and food for thought. The illustration at the top of page 12 shows how the elegant yet simply conceived gate and palisade fit into the context of the massive structure and heighten its effect. Our creations must evolve from the architectural style, so that together they form a unity, and here too we find good examples in work of the past (see the illustrations at the foot of page 12).

A piece of craftsmanship may also radiate humour – a fact which, regrettably, has almost been forgotten. The old masters often allowed themselves a touch of their own native brand of fun; and of course it is all to the good if, when looking at a piece of work, one can feel amused or even laugh. An occasional dash of humour is essential, just as in other circumstances austerity may be called for. Solid iron and humour may appear to be irreconcilable opposites, yet they can be combined.

It is said that Nature is the master of all masters. For our creative work, Nature provides us with an inexhaustible fund of suggestions, for Nature possesses the greatest abundance of designs. It is our task to convert them, with due attention to craftsmanship, into iron.

"To see a world in a grain of sand, and a heaven in a wild flower" – what marvels are contained in just the little things of Nature! Karl Blossfeldt showed in his book Urformen der Kunst greatly enlarged illustrations of parts of plants which were often in reality very small, and in so doing demonstrated that even in the smallest seed certain strict laws of design apply. But Karl Nierendorf, in his introduction to that book, rightly emphasized: "What distinguishes works of art from Nature is a result of the creative act: the character of an individual design newly created, not imitated or repeated. Art springs directly from the most prevalent dynamic force of the time, whose most visible expression it is." The aptness of Blossfeldt's work can be graphically illustrated. When designing a bar of a certain grille, I adopted a number of ideas suggested to me by a photograph in his book depicting a plant (see page 14). Such experiments in iron are necessary, even if there are no orders on hand for them, because they enrich one's stock of designs and can in due course be turned to good account by creating items of distinctive character. We can still admire many beautiful

Above: Gate, Regensburg
Cathedral.
Bottom, right:
Detail of above.
Bottom, left:
Part of a fountain screen in the
Cathedral grounds.

Balcony, the Palazzo Bevilaqua, Bologna.

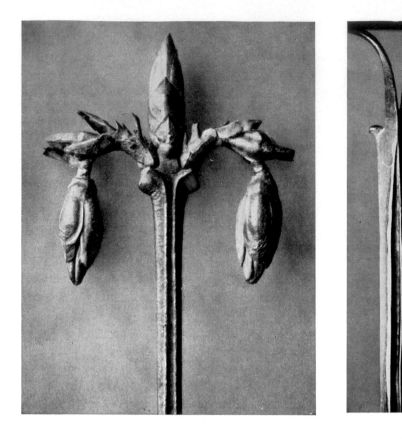

old works of craftsmanship and by studying them gain a wealth of ideas which in turn can be creatively applied. "New coins can be minted from fine old gold." A few works of the past are shown, in the illustrations on pages 12, 13, 15, 16 and 17. Judging the sizes of iron to be used for the various parts and their ratios one to another is a factor of special importance in the planning of a piece of work. The total effect often depends on this. Iron is a solid material, and the sectional sizes required for any given structure and its supports can be judged by experience. Why is iron used at all for, say, a grille? Firstly, because its strength provides excellent protection; and furthermore, a wrought-iron grille is comparatively light and enables one to see through it. Excessively heavy sections, especially if used without due regard to the proper uses of wrought ironwork, can easily give the finished article the appearance of wood. Any design which typifies another material is to be avoided. One should not, for instance, imitate in iron pillars which have been fashioned in wood, even going so far as to add a coat of paint. Even if made of iron, they will still resemble wooden pillars. Such misguided uses of materials, apparent for instance in the fashioning in wrought iron of designs intended for cast iron or plaster of Paris, regrettably occur far too often. On the other hand, wrought iron should never be made too weak and thin either. Iron must always remain iron.

Iron is always exposed to the danger of corrosion. To prevent this, smaller wrought-iron items designed for interiors are often given a black finish and then coated with a good colourless matt lacquer. This treatment, however, can never be applied to outdoor structures in wrought iron, as these will soon rust because of the weather; moist air alone is often enough to bring this about. Frequently when an order is placed for an outdoor structure a request is made to coat it with an appropriate finish, black being the colour most commonly specified. One can only call it ignorance if such treatment is insisted upon. Why exactly is this black finish wanted? One wants to be able to see by looking at the finished article how it was done – viz., that it was fashioned in wrought iron. The art of forging does not, however, consist in giving a black finish! We smiths are most reluctant to cover up our work with a protective coat of paint. It is much more important to us to know that a piece of work that has cost us a great deal of time and trouble is not heading for ruin but will be kept intact. The fact is that if, after a piece of wrought ironwork has been hammered to perfection, a coat of paint is applied, one's efforts have been largely wasted, for beneath the paint very little of the fine hammer-work remains visible. Many people have different views on this subject. Some say: "If all the iron were properly forged right through it would not rust." Others say: "The scale which is formed during forging protects the iron from rusting." And many take the view that it is a question of the iron itself – that in the past iron did not rust so readily, as may be seen by reference to surviving works. I would reply that there is doubtless something to be said for all these views, but I cannot, as suggested in the first instance, re-forge all the iron which I receive from the rolling-mill ready cut to definite lengths and thicknesses for, say, a large gate. This would only make the work considerably more expensive, and the iron would still rust when exposed to the elements for a short time. This is equally true for the second case. The third point I should like to answer by asking how it is that, relatively speaking, so few of the wrought-iron works of the past have survived to the present day. The answer lies precisely in the iron itself. I believe it is the wish of every smith who does decorative work to see every chemical and economic means at our disposal used to bring on the market a form of iron which, while possessing all the capabilities required for forging, is not expensive and does not rust. Many works of merit would then survive. As it is, for the time being we have to protect our work from rusting by applying a coat of paint and get the best results we can in design and colour from the material as we receive it. In this matter we smiths can perform an educational function. A good piece of wrought ironwork can be so conceived and fashioned as to give an entirely satisfactory result even when subjected to a protective coat of paint, provided that it is expertly applied.

Above:
Wrought ironwork on a terrace in Danzig.
Below:
Ironwork on a door of Nuremberg Castle.

Close attention must be paid to the rising generation of craftsmen. I have already referred to the importance of experimental designing, which makes a valuable contribution to one's development – for it is in this way that an ever-increasing collection of designs is built up by the craftsman. Such a collection serves both as advertisement and as a means of instructing apprentices. Our apprentices are undoubtedly more attentive and enthusiastic when they can see for themselves new designs continually evolving at the hands of a master-craftsman, and the way is thereby made smoother for them to progress to creative work of their own. The apprentice should be taught the basic prin-

Grille gate, Ambras Castle, Tirol.

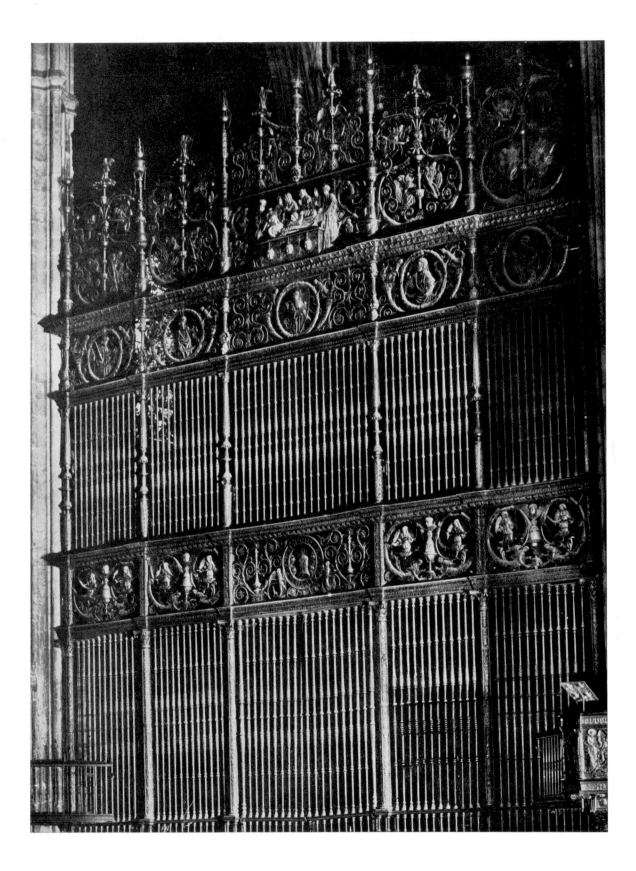

A réja (Spanish choir screen), Capilla Mayor, Seville.

Drawings help us to assess a projected piece of work and to ascertain how it will fit into the architecture. The illustration on the left shows a quick preliminary sketch (scale 1:10) for a tall wrought-iron door. It does not go into detail, but shows only the main features.

The illustration below is a quick rough sketch in charcoal (scale 1:1) which shows two figurative motifs. Even at the blueprint stage one must be clear about the execution. Such drawings can only be made by someone who has personal knowledge of forging.

The illustration on page 19, upper right, shows a charcoal drawing (scale 1:1) which serves do give the architect or building owner a rough idea of the plastic effect of the projected piece of work, and to establish, as far as possible, harmony with the main structure.

The other illustration on page 19 is a rough drawing for a large gateway and entrance gate (scale 1:10). It shows how the ironwork is to be incorporated into the wall and also, by means of the detail (scale 1:1), presents the architect with a clear picture of the design in close-up and its general effect.

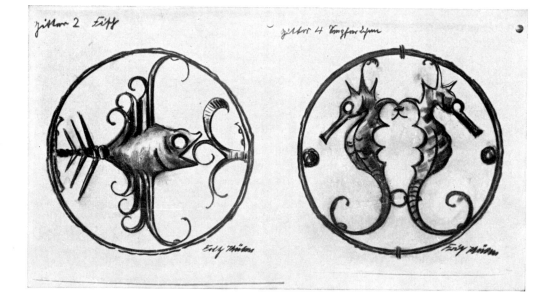

18

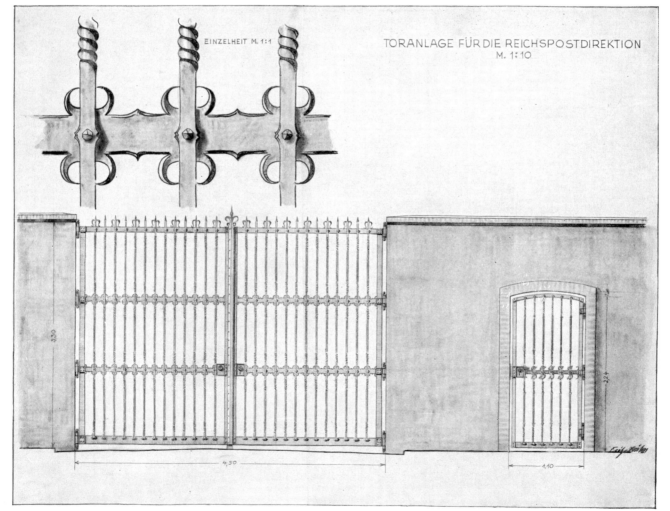

EINZELHEIT M. 1:1

TORANLAGE FÜR DIE REICHSPOSTDIREKTION
M. 1:10

ciples of his craft in such a way that the development of his creative faculties is made to keep pace with that of his technical capabilities. The prerequisite for this is of course that he is found to be a suitable person for such instruction. Attendance at technical schools is of great importance, even though the instruction there is bound to be confined more or less to basic principles. The proper acquisition of the craft can only be had in the workshop, through practical work undertaken with a positive and serious approach. Here the apprentice, like the journeyman, participates in the development of a piece of work from the blueprint stage to the working model and so on to the finished article. A clean and tidy workshop plays an important part in training (see illustration below). The basis for all future creative work is that one has properly mastered the craft. In art and architecture, indeed in life itself, craftsmanship must lead the way. It is a difficult but noble task to dedicate oneself wholly to one's craft and to make it one's aim in life to see that it is preserved for future generations. At this point, and in conclusion, I should like to thank once again all those who have contributed to my progress in my craft. Next to practical experience, which was my first teacher, I must mention first and foremost Professor Karl Schmidt, who took particular interest in me and trained me while I was a pupil of his at the Technical School in Berlin, where I attended evening classes; I have much to thank him for, both as a teacher and as a man. Also our doyen Julius Schramm was always a shining example to me.

At work.

Simple decorative design in bars of round and square section made by upsetting; the groove on the round bar is ribbed.

Ornamentation on bars of square and flat section formed by twisting the iron after it has been heated to a uniform bright red heat. The flat bar is grooved before twisting.

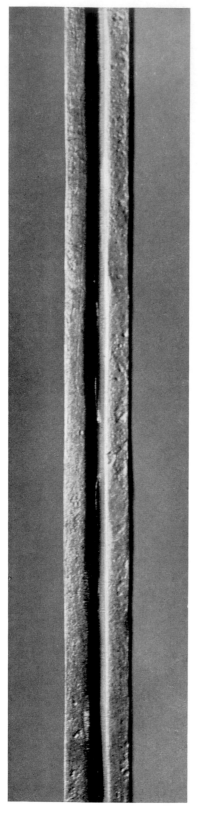

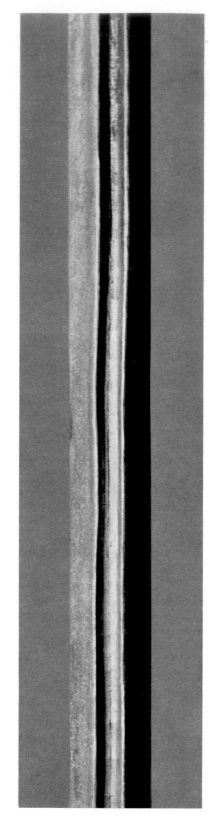

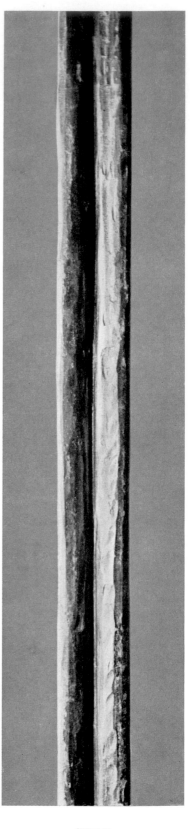

sharp-edged grooving

round grooving

profiled

Simple ornamentation of an iron bar.

Decorative design on a square bar. The scrolls are fitted into position on the bar by fire welding. The swelling at this joint shows the weld clearly.

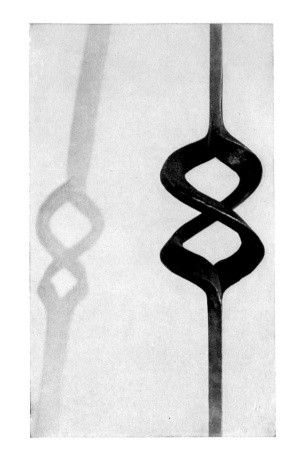

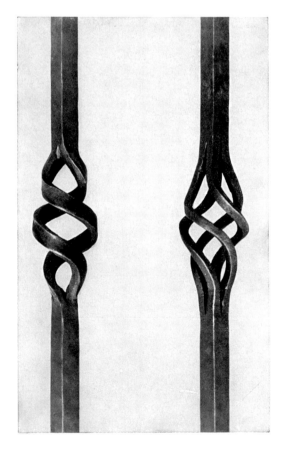

Imaginative designs applied to bars of square and flat section, achieved by opening out, upsetting, and twisting the iron.

Leaf forged in one piece; for solidity, the stem is not naturalistically round but flat and looped.

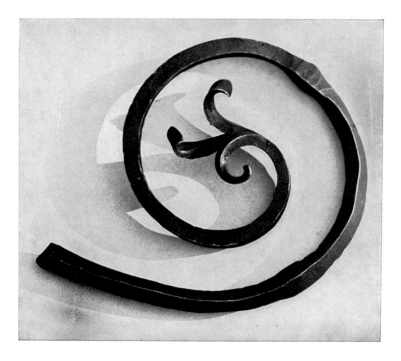

A tendril taken from Nature and transformed into wrought iron; the head is opened out.

Decorative design in a square bar, made in one piece by opening out and drawing out.

Variation of the same design. The natural surface, which can be clearly seen here,
was caused by heating and forging.

Decorative design in a square bar, made in one piece by opening out, upsetting and drawing out.

Decorative design on a square bar. The centre scrolls are opened out, the outer ones welded on.

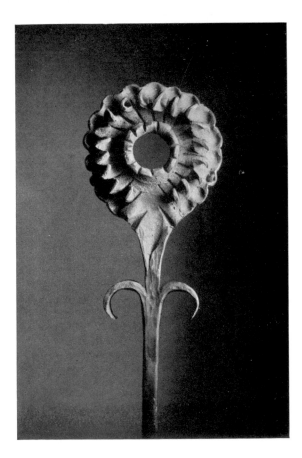

Flowers translated into the language of iron. All are fashioned from one piece.

Forged spike made from 1¹/₅-in. thick square bar. By opening up the scrolls the design was evolved naturally.

Decorative design of an intersection. At the point of intersection one of the bars is forged into a shallow U-shape to receive the other; they are then riveted. The scrolls are welded into position, and the bars grooved.

The fastening of the component parts was achieved by riveting; the horizontal bar is perforated and collared to allow the passage of the vertical bar (centre), and the tying is effected by means of collars.

A forged sign of the zodiac used as a figure for a clock. The grooves emphasize the lineal direction. The terminations are attenuated and drawn out broad. The sign is fastened to the wall by means of ornamentally forged rivets.

Detail from a grille. The intersections are overlapped, the rings opened out, the corners of the ornamental frame are upset and bent, grooved and rubbed bright. The vivid effect of this composition was achieved by working the iron while at a uniform bright red heat. The hammer-blows, which are clearly visible, were made during the forging process and the squaring-up. It is wrong to attempt to achieve such an effect by hammering the iron while cold or by 'squeezing-up'.

Method of fastening a tendril in wrought iron. Leaf and scroll are forged in one piece.

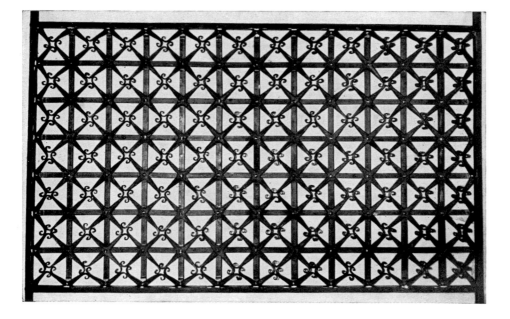

Close-textured screen, 4ft. 6in. × 2ft. 9in. The squared ironwork is made of flat bars $^{1}/_{4}$-in.×$^{1}/_{5}$-in., the intersections are bent over at right angles, the stars forged in one piece and riveted.

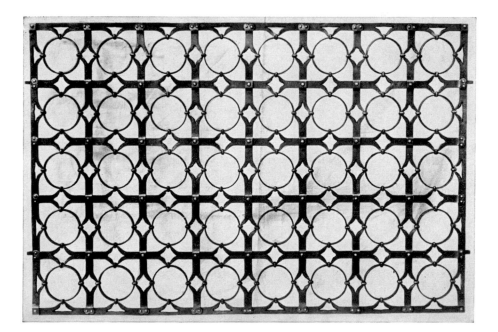

Screen, 4ft. 6in.×2ft. 9in. The squared ironwork is of $^7/_8$-in.×$^1/_4$-in. flat bar, the intersections are bent over at right angles, the rings are of $^5/_8$-in.×$^1/_4$-in. flat bar fastened to the opened-up pieces by collars.

Screen, 8ft. 6in. × 10ft. 9in. The bars are of $^3/_4$-in. square bar. Double horizontal rails keep the vertical bars at the correct distances, rivet points are emphasized by forged rosettes.

Partial view of a gate. The vertical members are of square bar, the horizontal rails of flat section with opened-out motifs, accentuated by the insertion of ornamental pieces.

Iron balusters, rings opened out and punched hollow. The method used for fastening the bars has here become an ornamental frieze. The bars were twisted at the centre under moderate heat.

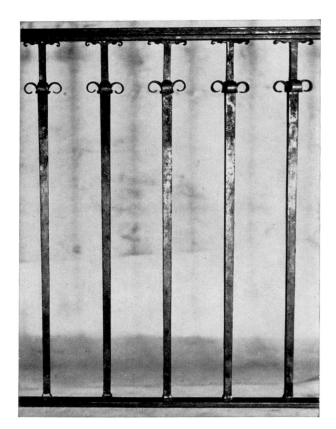

Railings. The scrolls of the decorative designs are opened out – that is to say, from the solid bar. The bars are tapered at the base.

Screen. The main construction is of $^1/_2$-in. thick square bar, the circular motifs of $^7/_8$-in. $\times$ $^1/_4$-in. flat iron. The ring with the protruding small scrolls is forged in one piece.

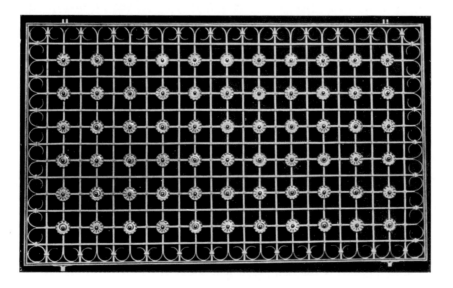

Screen of $^2/_5$-in. thick square bar, intersections punched hollow. For riveting the rosettes part of the intersections is overlapped. Rosettes of $^3/_{25}$-in. thick iron.

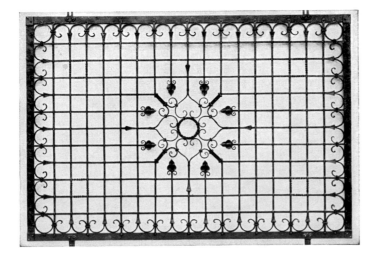

Screen. The scrolls are drawn out. The decorative
motif in the centre fans out from the trellis-work.

Gallery balustrade. The upper scrolls are hammered out to resemble leaves, the small scrolls at the swelling are opened out. The alternate rails are slightly grooved.

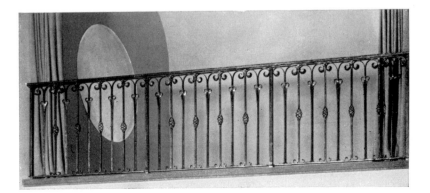

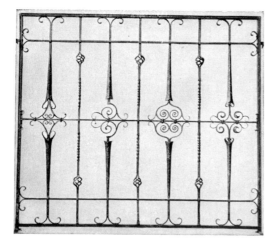

The variety of ornamentation enlivens this screen. The decorative motifs are in each case evolved from the bars.

Screen, ornamented with forged leaves of various shapes.
Both these and the scrolls are welded to the bar. The upper
and lower friezes are formed by opening-out of the bars.

Screen, 5ft.×3ft. This piece of work, and the one on the
facing page, demonstrate the use of broad and relatively
thin lengths of flat iron. The material for the decorative
motifs I achieved in both cases by drawing out.

Partial view of a double front gate, showing (right) the motifs.

Screen comprising three detachable panels. Grooved leaf, with scrolls in one piece, attached to the bar by fire welding. The bars are of flat section, alternately chamfered in front and adorned with half-twists.

Gilded balustrade for a music gallery. Swelling upset, bars grooved and then twisted.

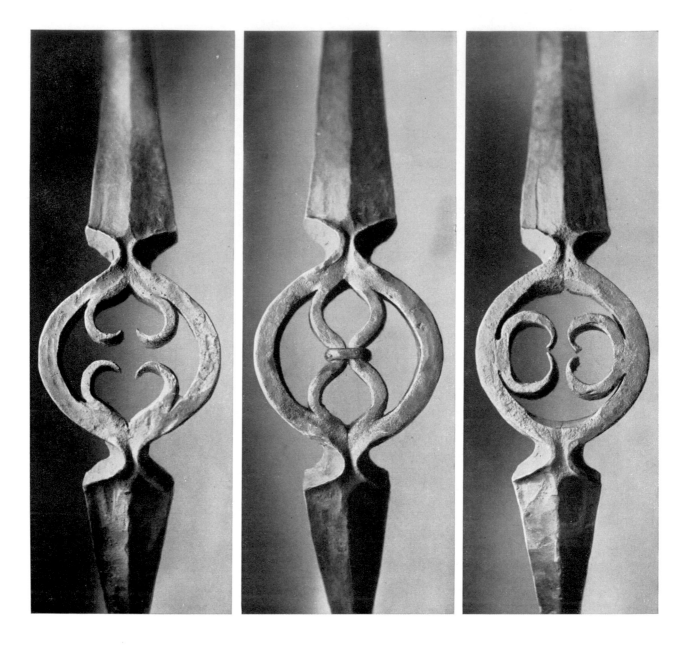

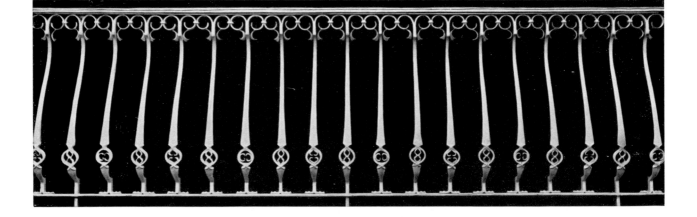

Gallery balustrade. Bars forged in one piece and bent forward. The decorative designs of the lower frieze were formed by drawing out and opening out.

Partition screen for a stage. Intersections punched hollow. The leaf-shaped terminations, which have been hammered out and convoluted, serve to strengthen the attachment to the frame. The distortion of the squares is rectified by the insertion of the flowers.

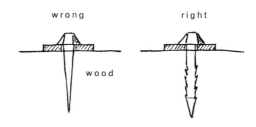

wrong   right

wood

Mounting on a door. The scrolls are drawn out. All intersections are riveted. The rivet-heads are forged and have small barbed hooks (see sketch). These can never fall out, even after the wood has dried out. The wood is rough-drilled before the rivets are hammered in.

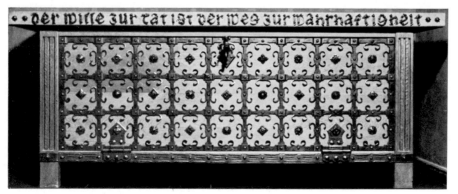

Book-chest, riveted throughout. All the large ornamental rivet-heads are different.

Partition screen in a public house.

60

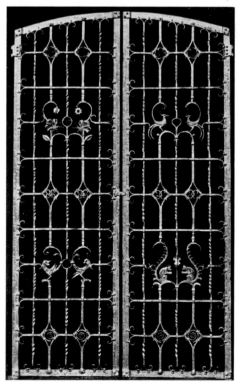

Double doors leading to a garden terrace. The animals are forged from one piece.

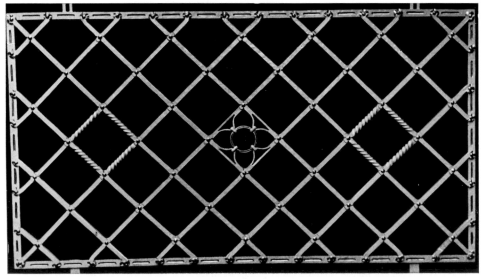

Screen with a simple centre ornament, achieved by drawing out and securing the ring by means of collars.

Gilded screen rubbed bright, with a lavish centre ornament fanning out from the trellis. The border of the frame is fluted.

Double doors with centre ornament.

Panel with coat of arms.

The effectiveness of this panel lies in the simple division into squares. The only refinement in this example of wrought ironwork is the swelling of the intersections, caused by the punchings. The illustration below shows the development of a punching from the initial to the final stage.

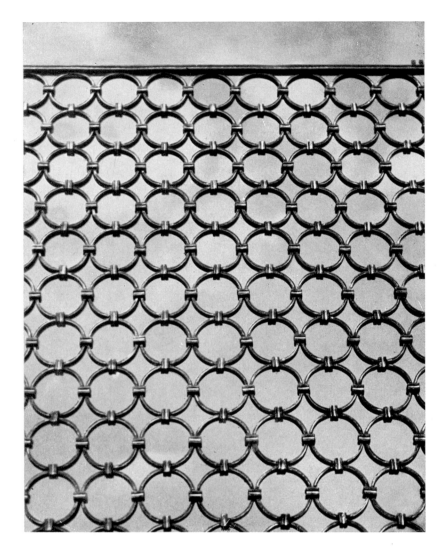

This piece of wrought ironwork is formed by a recurrent sequence of rings. The interruption of this sequence by means of strengthening collars enlivens the otherwise flat appearance. The rings and collars are grooved. The rings are welded together. The lower illustration shows the preliminary work at the welding point.

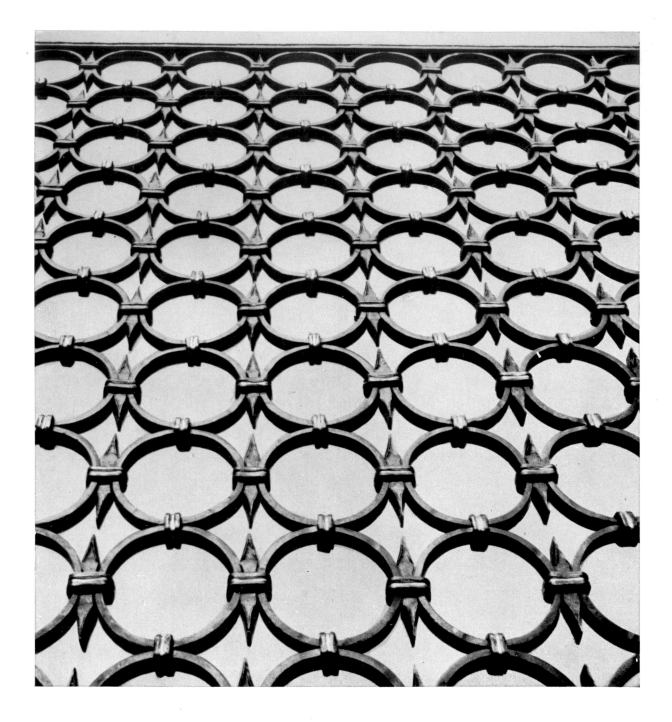

Partial view of a large screen. By means of the alternate wedge-shaped components the whole achieves verticality. The collars are grooved.

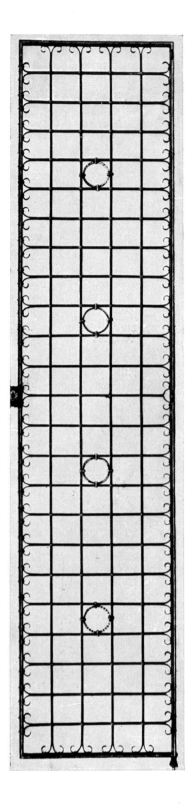

Wrought-iron door, 10ft. 6in. high, the intersections punched hollow, the terminations drawn out.
The collared rings are fashioned in various designs – namely, with sharp-edged grooving, twisted,
with sharp-edged and round grooving.

70

In both these examples motifs taken from Nature have been transformed into wrought iron. The bars in both examples are of flat section, the leaves welded on, the scrolls in the example on the left drawn out.

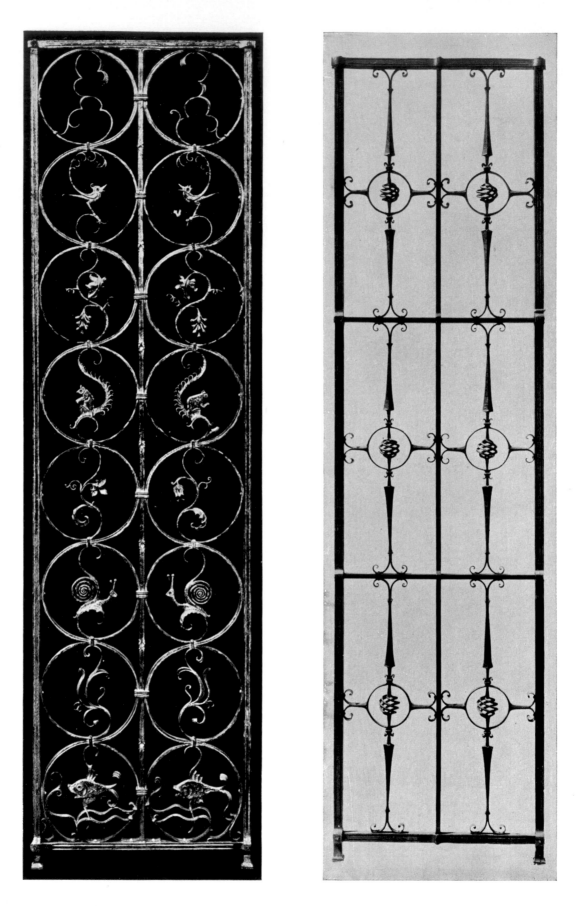

Two screens 10ft. 6in. high. The one on the left, designed for a spacious interior, is gilded; deriving its inspiration from Nature, it gives a festive atmosphere to the room. The one on the right, designed for outdoor use, is correspondingly more austere.

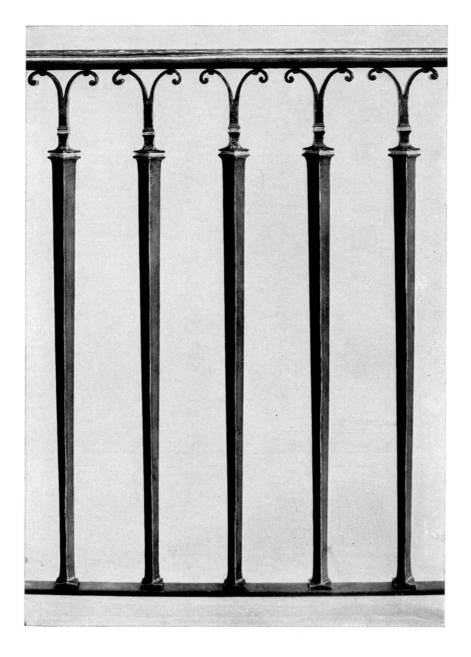

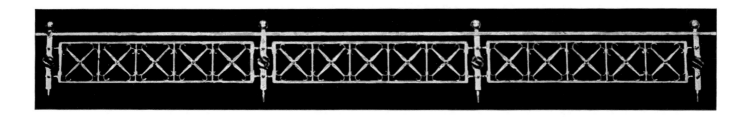

Above: Part of a wrought-iron balcony. The bars are in one piece, the grooves gilded.
Below: Low gallery balustrade, gilded.

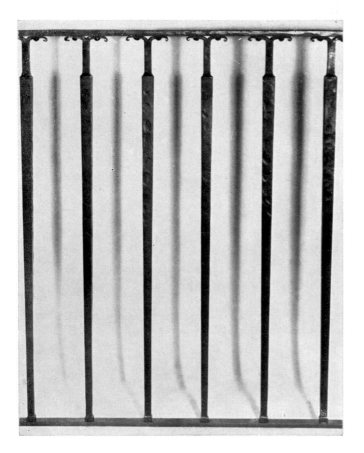

Parapet, severely simple. The bars are in one piece
and tapered at the base.

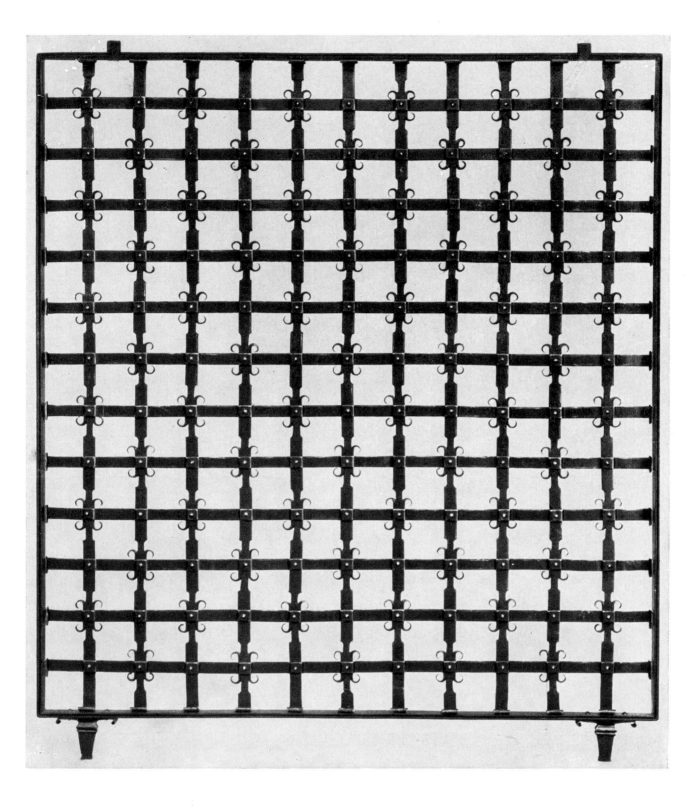

Screen made up of squares from thin bars of flat section; the intersections are bent over at right angles and riveted. The small ornaments are drawn out.

Ornamentation inserted into wrought ironwork, symbolizing the craft.

Another symbol.

A front gate incorporating the family crest. The individual letters forming
the name and the leaping horse are each forged from one piece.

Screen for a building by the sea.

Detail from the entrance to a bowling alley.
Detail from a fanlight incorporating the elements water and air.

Detail of a partition screen for a public house.

Figurative motifs as wall decoration
or as ornamental features in
wrought ironwork.

These amusing creatures form an appropriately designed and well-integrated composition with the circle.

Detail of a fish forged in iron.

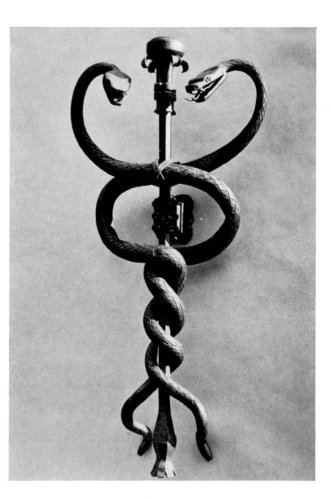

Aesculapius's staff, the snakes of thick iron of round section each forged from one piece, the head opened out.

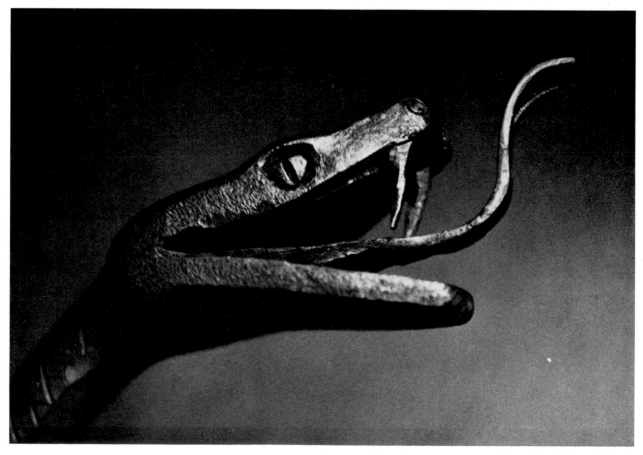

Opening in a wall.

Wing of a double gate and porter's gate.

Two gateways.

88

Partial view of a gate. The diamond-shaped trellis-work is riveted to the frame.
Left: View through a gate. Ornamental and fastening devices achieved by opening out.

A 20ft. wide double entrance gate. The gate shows that is technically possible to manage without diagonal supports, though only the absolutely necessary minimum sections of iron bar were used. In this way a clear view beyond is obtained. The detail shows the points of attachment.

This photograph shows that an effective result is nevertheless obtained.
By means of the twists a handsome frieze effect is achieved.

91

Protective grille on the front
window of a tenement house.

Wrought-iron door in a dining-room, leading to the garden terrace.

Two panels on a staircase.

Gilded radiator screen in a reception hall.

Radiator screen in an ante-room; the grooves are gilded.

Parapet rails on a music gallery in a large hall.
Balustrade of a concert hall stage.

Gallery balustrade in a banqueting hall.

Iron banisters.

Iron banisters.

Stair ramps in a business house. With a black finish relieved by gilt.

Clock dial on a school building.

Wrought-iron hinges for wooden doors.

Entrance door of a public house.

Iron mountings on a double door.
The smaller photograph shows the motif in greater detail.

Screen in a public house.

Grate and fire-irons.

Grate support. The globe, forged from one piece, is of square bar.

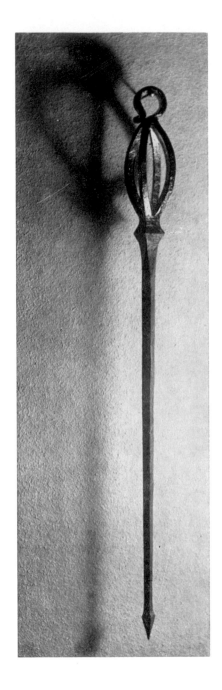

Poker and shovel, each forged from one piece.

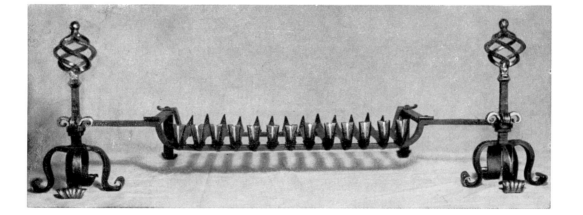

Fireplace equipment.

Weather-vane.

Clock dial.

Craftsman – detail
from a crowning piece.

Heavy candlestick.

Table with candelabrum and dish.
Table legs forged from one piece.

LIGHT METAL

The widespread use of aluminium nowadays for the type of work we do prompts me to include here a few examples and to say something about the subject.

Light metal is nowadays available in various alloys and can be used for both grilles and other objects, but allowances must be made for the properties of this material, which differ in certain basic respects from those of iron, particularly in structure and colour. It is true that, technically, light metal can be worked like iron; but it is questionable whether designs forged in iron can be applied to this other medium. For aesthetic reasons alone this would not be desirable. Moreover, aluminium has a less solid character than iron, and for this reason more stable designs must be chosen. It must also be noted that colour influences design. Just as gold, silver and bronze are given designs appropriate to their individual character, so too must designs for light metal be made appropriate to its character. To use aluminium for typical iron motifs, and perhaps go so far as to give it a black finish, is wrong. One must on principle guard against simulating decorative wrought ironwork in other materials. For light-metal work I consider the utilization of such modern techniques as grinding, oxy-acetylene welding, filing, milling and polishing – all vindicated by the great advantages they can claim – to be entirely right and proper, since we are dealing here with a modern material.

To make light metal resistant to corrosion and to maintain its colour, the eloxal process (anodic oxidation) is widely used. This is a process of coating aluminium or aluminium alloys with a layer consisting essentially of aluminium oxide. The anodized surface can be coloured with various aniline dyes if desired. But not all aluminium alloys can be treated in like fashion, and due care must therefore be taken in selecting. Apart from the natural tones, nickel-silver, brass and bronze tones, as well as other colours, can be obtained. The natural and nickel-silver tones are, however, to be preferred to the others, as they are appropriate to the character of aluminium, particularly in regard to artistic works.

It is therefore entirely possible to produce from light metal good, craftsmanlike works which will contribute to the beauty of a building.

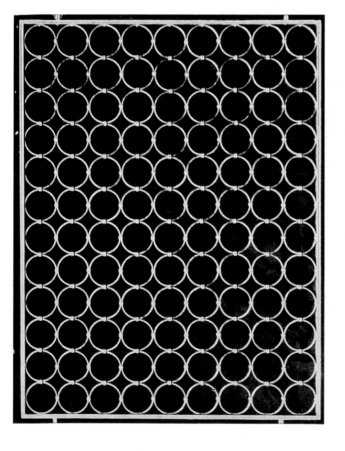 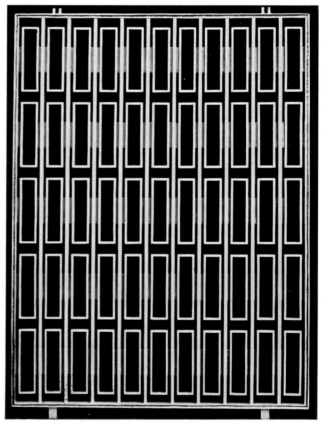

Aluminium screens. The illustration on the left shows the effect in the room.

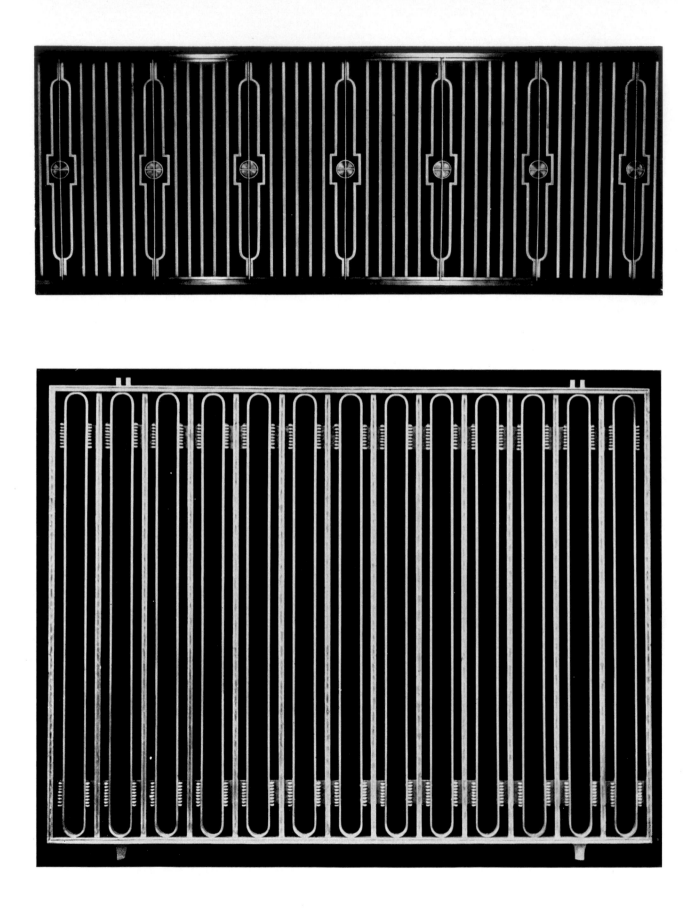

Aluminium balustrade and screen.

Light-metal balustrade nickel-silver in tone, the leaves and small globes finished in a
bright golden tone by anodizing them.

Iron dish incorporating family crest.